Book 7 in the Dece

OUR JOURNEY FOR DIVERSITY AND INCLUSION IN BUSINESS

Blueprint for all and Healthy Leadership CIC

PREFACE

Dear Colleagues, welcome to this workbook. Many of us have been working for a world that is inclusive of all, regardless of difference and some of us have made progress in the sectors in which we operate.

But it is time to do more. Then we will leave an honourable legacy for those who follow us. We will enact Dr Martin Luther King's dream of a blueprint for all. We will create working environments that allow people to 'be the best of whatever you are.' Where people have a deep belief in their own dignity and worth and they always feel that they count. (Extracts from a speech made by Dr Martin Luther King to high school students. Barratt Junior High School, Philadelphia, USA, October 26th, 1967).

We provide a way for you to review your readiness to explore your own approach to diversity, equity, and inclusion (DE&I). This is a method for you and your organisation to review your current efforts. Finally, we present you with a range of interventions from which to choose to further develop your organisation and thus make a greater contribution to our quest for inclusion.

Thank you
Sonia and Anna

Sonia Watson, OBE, Chief Executive, Blueprintforall
Anna Eliatamby, Director, Healthy Leadership, CIC

GLOSSARY

Diversity, equity, and inclusion

Rosencrance (2022) describes diversity, equity, and inclusion (DE&I) as a term developed to describe policies, strategies, and other interventions to promote the representation and inclusion of groups who may have been previously excluded. Diversity is a collective term used to describe differences -both overt and covert.

Diversity is "any dimension that can be used to differentiate groups and people from one another" ("What is Diversity," 2019). Therefore, diversity issues in the workplace are not just limited to race and ethnicity but should include everything from sexuality to physical and intellectual ability, religion, age, gender, culture, and anything that could differentiate a person as "other" in a group.

In the United Kingdom (UK), we know these qualities as protected characteristics, as defined by the UK Equality and Human Rights Commission and the Equalities Act of 2010. They include age, disability, gender reassignment, marriage and civil partnership, pregnancy and maternity, race, religion or belief, sex, and sexual orientation. Mental health is also considered. Other jurisdictions also include socioeconomic status, skills, and expertise.

The aim of equity is to ensure that there is fair access, justice, and impartiality for all to all available goods and services and parts of an organisation. We achieve this by understanding the underlying contributory factors.

The purpose of equity is the inclusion of those who are diverse. This should occur, without exception, for all employees of an organisation. The work environment should be inclusive, supportive, and respectful. Staff who require extra supports, e.g. physical aids should have access to them. Factors that hinder and facilitate DE&I are identified, understood, and addressed where necessary.

Intersectionality

Crenshaw (1989) first used the term intersectionality to describe the fact that African American women experienced cumulative forms of discrimination-racism and sexism. The term is now used to refer to how differences intersect and overlap. Thus, for the individual, their negative and positive experiences are often a result of these overlaps rather than because of a single difference. Roos (2022).

Toxicity

This is a commonly used term to describe the negative aspects of the behaviours shown in an organisation. Toxic behaviours include bullying, harassment, discrimination, lying, fraud, and corruption. They vary in intensity, severity, frequency, and impact. Unfortunately, these negative behaviours are often used to target diverse people in an organisation.

Psychological safety

Schein and Bennis (1965) were one of the first to use the term psychological safety. They described it as "an atmosphere where one can take chances (which experimentalism implies) without fear and with sufficient protection". These cultures encourage trust, openness, and lead to a loss of fear by employees. As a result, they become more productive and engage at higher levels.

CONTENTS

INTRODUCTION

In 2022, we reviewed research on the work that has been done in organisations to facilitate DE&I. There have been various efforts across the world, some have been successful, but the research shows that we have much more to do.

There are a few organisations who have been successful in achieving significant levels of inclusion in all the ways that matter. For example, those that are gender diverse outperform others by 15%. Pew Centre research (2019) shows 45% of those surveyed in various countries are in favour of a more diverse society. However, 23% did not consider it a necessity. Poushter, Fetterrolf et al. (2019).

The Messenger and Pollard report of leadership in the UK NHS (2022) clearly found that there was still a lack of inclusion, discrimination, and a failure to provide psychological safety. This is a common finding and therefore an indictment that, regardless of sector, we still produce reports with the same results even after twenty years. What do we need to bring about the required change? Leadership must be courageous and take the risks for inclusion to work.

As a society, we also have much to do, as evidenced by the frequent reports of the presence of discrimination in our societies and communities. Even when a diverse person publicly recounts their experience of discrimination, there will be those who describe them as woke, refuse to honour the veracity of their experience and are sometimes inappropriate, "well, everyone goes through this, so why are you complaining?". Even when the diverse person has described an awful experience.

While it is laudable that there has been a variety of initiatives, there is much left to do. Diversity and awareness training have an impact, at least in the short term. What is not clear is if subsequent shifts in behaviour back the statements made by attendees that they have changed their views. While some businesses have a diversity strategy, fewer have set clear goals and targets.

So, what do we need to do? We have noted three barriers in the research: of the work environment, people themselves and the quality of diversity initiatives. Other factors include toxicity, poor attitudes towards inclusion, unconscious bias, and workplace culture. Further details of the research we reviewed and reported above are in the Appendix.

We used the findings to build a method for you to explore safely your current attitude to DE&I and your organisation's approach. We then offer a range of interventions for you to consider. You can adapt the reflections for use with groups, even though we focus on the individual.

READINESS FOR THE EXPLORATION

The most important intervention for us to consider, as we discuss the journey to inclusion, is our own readiness and attitudes. As fair as we think are, we can always stop and reflect. Even those of us who have worked in diversity should not assume that we have no biases and perspectives that could get in the way. For example, saying that you treat everyone equally but then suddenly realising that you prefer people who have academic qualifications which has meant that you have missed someone's natural intelligence. You have also missed the fact that they may not have had the same opportunities as you did.

For us to consider inclusion, we need to prepare ourselves for this exploration. It may not be easy to give yourself that permission. If it is not the right time, then please stop and wait. Perhaps think about who you could talk to and become ready or just wait until it is the right time.

Speaking to a coach or someone who is diverse can make a difference. We were running a session on diversity awareness for very senior professionals and most of them were finding it difficult to accept that their business economy discriminated against diverse colleagues. Until one of the diverse facilitators recounted experiences that one of their relatives had gone through. This then led to a shift in the session's atmosphere and the intentions of the participants.

If you choose to wait, please create a quiet hour for yourself. Find a place and time in which you can relax. Then think about why you want to wait and what or who could support you while you are waiting. It is best to choose people who will help you but will not unnecessarily challenge.

If you want to explore, then there are some suggestions below. As adults and successful professionals, we have a repertoire of attitudes and behaviours built over the years, and of course, they work for us or so we like to think. Rarely do we give ourselves the psychological and practical space to pause and reflect. Let's start the journey.

First, think about your **approach to change**. We dislike change, especially if it is not our choice, e.g. if it is an emergency.

The path of change

The diagram describes the process of change that people take. The first step to think about is how ready you are to change. Where would you locate yourself on the left-hand axis of the graph? Now, consider the various actions and emotions that people go through on their change journey.

If you are ready, how do you change? Which steps do you take and in what order?

If you are resistant, what do you do? Which steps do you take and in what order?

What can help you shift from being resistant or reluctant towards being ready?

What will motivate you to maintain this shift?

Now, please use your learning from the above task and apply it to your approach to diversity.

How would you describe your current attitudes, emotions, and behaviours towards DE&I? What would you like your future approach to be? How open are you to this proposed change? What do you need to help you on your change journey? How willing are you to take the risks to enhance DE&I?

You can easily adapt this reflection for use with a group. It is highly unlikely that there will be synergy in the paths of change that individuals will take. But that is worth knowing. Some may explore, and others could be extremely reluctant. If there is resistance, then it is worth considering how you can understand this so that people become more ready to explore. Rarely is it worth mandating such actions. If you do and people are unwilling, then you could encounter sabotage. If there is overall willingness, then consider what they need to support the group throughout the process.

Please note down your learning here.

My learning

If you are ready to proceed, then get a notebook you can use on your journey through the reflections in the book.

UNDERSTANDING OF DIVERSITY AND DIFFERENCE

It is always useful to look at our history to learn about how and where we developed our views, perspectives, and the associated behaviours. Here are some reflections for you to use.

You can conduct these in private, or with a trusted person. You could also use them with a group.

Remember to prepare by noting that this can be uncomfortable but necessary. Be patient with yourself as you learn.

It isn't necessary that you carry out all the reflections. Please try to use at least two.

OPENNESS TO DIVERSITY, EQUITY, AND INCLUSION

Reflect on what you learned above about your approach to DE&I. Think of yourself in the last month. Which words and thoughts did you use? What do people say about your approach to DE&I? How comfortable are you with your conclusions? Where would you locate yourself in this diagram?

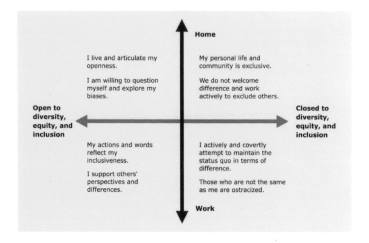

If you are going to use this with a group, then it is best to prepare them for the reflection. It is also entirely possible that you will not achieve congruence across the group. That, itself, may be the learning.

WHAT AND WHO HAS INFLUENCED ME OVER THE YEARS?

Stop, find a quiet place and time to do this reflection. It may be helpful for you to gather some pictures and memories so you can comfortably review your history.

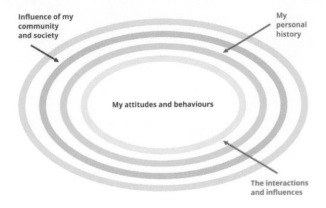

Using the diagram above, think about your attitudes and behaviours towards difference. Just write them down. Now think about personal history and the influence of your community and society in terms of diversity and equity. What were the prevalent attitudes and perspectives? Then think about how these have influenced you. Positively or negatively?

Look for explanations of your current approach to diversity and inclusion. What have you noticed? What did you miss? Imagine what a diverse person would say about what you have written.

You could adapt this to use with groups in your organisation. The focus could be on the organisational culture and attitudes and behaviours. Describe them and look at the organisational history and the impact of the wider local community and society. Remember to include those of the employees. Then reflect on what the influences have been and therefore what is the learning.

Please note down what you have realised and learned in your notebook.

My learning

HOW DO I USE MY PRIVILEGE, POWER, AND POSITION?

Our positions and roles, as senior people, bestow privilege, power, and position. These can also occur because of the social or cultural group to which we belong. For example, where we live, the school or university we went to, our accent, our ethnicity. These can influence us and provide us with greater privilege and power. And therefore, some may assume that they are more powerful than they are. Occasionally, we can also use or misuse these privileges.

For example, letting people know you studied at a prestigious university or did a leadership course at one of the premier institutions such as INSEAD. This is an intention to show superiority and to subjugate.

It is worth exploring this facet to learn more about how you utilise your privilege, power, and position.

Here are some **scenarios**. What would you do?

Someone who went to the same university and with whom you have stayed in touch has told you that their daughter has applied for a job in your organisation. You agree to investigate. You learn the candidate is third on the shortlist post interview and the position is still open. The first choice has declined the offer. You know and like the daughter.

A colleague, with whom you worked with ten years ago, has been accused of bullying diverse staff. You are surprised as you did not observe this except that the colleague once or twice refused to be in meetings with another organisation whose chief executive was diverse. They did not properly explain why. You contacted HR and learned about what has happened. The HR director, also diverse, has said that there is substantial evidence against the colleague. The colleague, another senior executive like you, approaches you and says that none of it is true and asks for your help.

Two team members who say that they have evidence that you dislike them have given you feedback, including that you do not listen to their perspectives.

MY PRIVILEGE, POWER, AND POSITION.

Write all the words that come to mind when you think of privilege, power, and position, both negative and positive. Which words would you use to describe yourself? Which words would staff you manage choose? Compare the two lists. What have you noticed? What does this say about your use of your privilege, power, and position?

Please note down your learning in your notebook.

My learning

Again, these reflections can be altered to use with a group, e.g., an executive board. However, they must share with each other. If there is reluctance, then think about how people could do the reflection separately but then provide honest feedback to the larger group.

IN MY ORGANISATION

Now it is time to consider the efforts made by your organisation. We have based this process on the research (in the Appendix) and the guidance provided by the International Standard for Diversity, Equity, and Inclusion. This contains a much more detailed process than the one described below. You can use this instead of the one we have devised.

There are a variety of approaches that can investigate. You could use an extensive review of both quantitative and qualitative data. For example, you could look at your DE&I strategy and review what progress there has been, consider the number of complaints, staff attrition and retention.

Qualitative methods include focus groups using the questions below are an option. You could utilise pulse surveys.

Regardless of the methods you choose, it is important to model inclusion by asking staff to be part of the design and review. In this way, you are more likely to get change post investigation.

STEPS TO TAKE

Select a group that represents the organisation. Then agree how you will help and support each other as you conduct the review.

Choose the key areas (see below) that you feel need to be investigated. Ideally, choose all of them, but that can make it a time-consuming process.

Agree the methodologies that you will use.

Carry out the review.

Present the findings in an open and honest manner to as many of the employees as possible. Ask for their views and suggestions on how to praise where there has been success and what they should do to address issues or problems.

Create a plan of action. You could use our suggestions below.

KEY AREAS

Area
Organisational culture, attitudes, and definitions
Governance and leadership
Learning and development

| Internal justice system |
| Human resource management life cycle |
| Operational policies and strategies |
| Products, services, development and design, procurement and supply chains, and external stakeholder relationships. |

Here are some questions you could ask.

A) Organisational culture, attitudes, and definitions

What is our definition of diversity, equity, and inclusion?

What behaviours and attitudes do we show in our organisation to reflect positive and negative approaches to diversity, equity, and inclusion?

What other positive and toxic behaviours do we show? How are toxic behaviours dealt with? What do we do to reinforce the use of positive actions?

What types of discrimination are present or reported?

To what extent is our organisational culture supportive of diversity, equity, and inclusion?

What do we do to include or exclude diverse staff?

How much are psychological safety and trust present?

What and who supports or blocks inclusion and diversity, equity, and inclusion?

How prepared are we to be courageous and take risks to address problems related to diversity, equity, and inclusion?

B) Governance and leadership

How do our governance and leadership systems facilitate diversity, equity, and inclusion?

What impedes inclusion?

What do we do to ensure that we incorporate DE&I in our operations, policies, and strategies?

What goals and outcomes do we have for DE&I?

How effective are senior personnel in modelling inclusion and how consistently?

How prepared is the leadership to be courageous and take risks to address problems related to diversity, equity, and inclusion?

What do we do to promote collective accountability–promoting the positive and openly encouraging the addressing of toxicity?

C) Learning and development

What education and training are available to encourage staff to review their approaches and attitudes to DE&I and then embed the learning in daily practice?

How are DE&I incorporated into generic learning and development?

What do we do to ensure that there is behavioural change post courses?

How do we support the overall development and progress of diverse staff?

D) Internal justice system

Some organisations will have an internal justice system that permits staff to raise any concerns about how they have been treated. These systems usually include a reporting mechanism (sometimes anonymous), a process for confidential investigation and an ombuds or mediation and dispute resolution service. Staff representatives and a staff welfare or well-being unit usually supplement these. The justice system often reports directly and confidentially to the most senior person in the organisation and is separate from the human resources function.

What is in place, and how effective is it?

How much do staff trust the system?

What has been the learning?

E) Human resource management life cycle: workforce planning, remuneration, recruitment, onboarding, learning and development, performance management, succession planning, workforce mobility and cessation of employment.

How do these facilitate equity, inclusion, and diversity?

What are the barriers?

How often are these reviewed for impact in relation to equity and diversity?

How well do we ensure the well-being of our staff? What support systems are in place?

What help are diverse staff given if they experience discrimination?

What help do we give to those who use discriminatory or toxic behaviours?

F) Operational policies and strategies

How do these support the vision for inclusion, diversity, and equity?

G) Products, services, development and design, procurement and supply chains, and external stakeholder relationships.

What do we do to ensure we are inclusive in our work and products?
What are our standards for working with third parties and external stakeholders?

CREATING A LEGACY FOR INCLUSION, EQUITY, AND DIVERSITY

Gather your findings and review them with all concerned. What has been positive and should be celebrated? What should you address? Give people time to digest the results. Then consider what will be your next steps.

It may help to review exactly where you are in terms of progress for DE&I using the levels below, which outline an organisation and its progress towards DE&I.

Level One- no significant interventions in place to promote DE&I and negative attitudes are present. Diverse staff just survive in the organisation.

Level Two- a few interventions introduced, little is done to address the negativity or to support implementation. Diverse staff only speak up if they have no other option. Most leave if they can.

Level Three- key interventions are in place and operationalised. Leadership and staff promote a positive attitude. Diverse staff feel included.

Level Four- there is synergy across key interventions. Leadership models appropriate behaviours and is extremely supportive. Diverse staff contribute to all DE&I initiatives.

Inevitably, it may not be possible to provide an overall rating given the likely variability of interventions and effectiveness across the organisation. Here, you may choose to allocate a range of levels to the different intervention areas.

Having done so, it is time to create your legacy statement and plan.

Think about the legacy you want to leave as a leader and as an organisation. What will be your core purpose and intention? Think about your definition of diversity? How much do you want to embrace intersectionality? How would you like to be remembered? For example,

Our legacy is that everyone feels part of and not separate from the rest of the workforce.

We model and live inclusion.

All will do our very best to be inclusive. We will celebrate our successes, be honest about our failures, and address them. We will enable, not stifle voices.

Select and prioritise your key focus areas. Now, with the core group, generate actions for the future. You could use our suggestions below.

Please make sure that the actions and goals you create contain challenge and yet are realistic. Remember to make sure that the work for inclusion by individuals and the organisation is consistent and day to day and not forgotten in the massive agenda you have.

Area	Prioritisation	Key action, goals with timeframes and support requirements.
Celebration of our achievements		
Organisational culture, attitudes and definitions		
Governance and leadership		
Learning and development		
Internal justice system		

Human resource management life cycle		
Operational policies and strategies		
Products, services, development and design, procurement and supply chains, and external stake-holder relationships		

Here are some suggestions for you.

Area	Suggestions
Celebration of our achievements	Offer opportunities to celebrate successes and efforts made to enhance inclusion.
Organisational culture, attitudes, and definitions	Provide mechanisms for regular feedback from staff about DE&I. Offer education opportunities, including training, secondment around diversity. Ensure that the learning is applied and leads to behavioural change. Create an organisational culture of openness and inquiry by example. Encourage collective accountability -where there is praise and recognition of the positive and openly report and address problems linked to DE&I and toxicity.

Governance and leadership	Ensure that the governance and leadership reflect diversity in terms of presence, guidance, and behaviours. Leadership promotes collective accountability. All should model consistently the expected behaviours.
	Develop and implement a clear DE&I strategy with goals, objectives, and timelines. Allocate personnel to this implementation with sufficient time to fulfil these duties. They should possess the requisite skills and knowledge and be willing participants.
Learning and development	Give opportunities for all to learn in formal and informal settings. Provide training with follow up, e.g., via coaching to embed the learning. Possible topics include exploring approaches to DE&I, recognising, and addressing bias, learning how to resolve misunderstanding and conflict in terms of diversity and inclusion, learning how to understand each other's communication.
	Encourage staff to work together and learn from each other.
	Provide networks for diverse staff with adequate resources and time.

Internal justice system	Establish or improve the existing internal justice system so that it is operational and trusted. Elements should include a reporting mechanism, investigation arm and mediation and dispute resolution process, adequate staff representation and staff welfare, counselling, and support.
Human resource management life cycle	All human resources processes for the life cycle are inclusive of all differences for current and prospective employees. All systems are confidential and HR staff is trusted and inclusive.
Operational policies and strategies	All policies are proactive and updated regularly to promote DE&I. Provide those in charge of implementation with opportunities to learn and reflect on the actions they have taken.
Products, services, development and design, procurement and supply chains, and external stakeholder relationships.	Take care to ensure that all these elements reflect the legacy statement. Select partners and stakeholders that reflect the intentions of the DE&I strategy and the legacy statement.

Thank you for your time. We wish you the best. Please contact us if you have questions.

https://www.blueprintforall.org/

https://healthyleadership.world/

APPENDIX

RESEARCH REPORT: FACTORS THAT HINDER AND FACILITATE DIVERSITY, EQUITY, AND INCLUSION

ACKNOWLEDGEMENTS

Brittany White produced this report for Blueprint for all and Healthy Leadership CIC. Copyright and ownership remain with both organisations.

Further material is available on the respective websites:

https://www.blueprintforall.org/

https://healthyleadership.world/

Please reference and use the material respectfully.

CONTENTS

INTRODUCTION

Our world is diverse and there is a greater recognition of this and the need to ensure inclusivity with respect. Businesses have, for some years, introduced a range of diversity initiatives and programmes. We review these and provide background information to relevant issues linked to implementing DE&I- both blocks and factors that help. We then make a range of suggestions.

This summary of research and seminal guidance includes a range of studies from recent to older ones when relevant. As much as possible, we focused on findings for the United Kingdom, but included other jurisdictions as needed.

We adopted an inclusive approach to the definition of difference to incorporate as many facets and qualities as possible so that we addressed the need for intersectionality in business. DE&I is an organisational intention for any person or group who has a declared or (sometimes) undeclared difference. This includes, but is not exclusive to, the protected characteristics mentioned earlier.

We refer to toxicity in organisations. A toxic work environment is one where negative behaviour occurs and is permitted. These actions have a negative impact on colleagues, and they often affect the viability and productivity of an organisation.

The terms used to describe this field and associated endeavours have developed as the arena has grown, from equality to diversity to now DE&I. The intentions for equity and inclusion remain.

Through working for diversity and equity, we hope to achieve inclusion. There are levels of inclusion from the presence of people with differences but who remain as 'outsiders' to true involvement and engagement of diverse people in the organisation and a culture and structure that supports DE&I.

However, a lack of successful diversity initiatives and implementation in society is still very much a current issue. Many examples come to mind. Articles in the media, recounting incidents of racism, sexism, and homophobia are still common. Adopting diversity initiatives alone does not guarantee a positive or expected outcome in society or the workplace.

Companies with an inclusive culture thrive. Those with the greatest diversity in racial and ethnic groups are more likely to have greater financial returns than average by 35% ("Working in Diverse," n.d.). Gender-diverse companies are also more likely to outperform by 15%. However, the haphazard introduction of diversity policies that are not then implemented can lead to more harm than good. To know how to implement diversity in both the workplace and social spaces, we must first understand the associated issues.

"Identity exclusion, stereotyping, and implicit bias, among other barriers, play a role, and, together with an inequitable distribution of opportunities and resources, produce and reproduce racial and gendered inequalities. Identifying barriers to inclusion and understanding how they shape behaviour is critical to eliminating them" (Grindstaff, 2022).

A BRIEF HISTORY OF DIVERSITY, EQUITY, AND INCLUSION

DE&I in the workplace became popular as interventions in the 1960s after introducing both affirmative action and equal employment laws to the justice system in the United States (Dong, 2021) as well as other countries, including the United Kingdom. This coincides with what is widely known as the second wave of feminism, which focused on equal pay and employment opportunities for women, and civil rights and equality legislation in many jurisdictions. In the late 1900s, however, businesses were more concerned with using diversity training to protect themselves against civil rights suits than they were in implementing DE&I into the culture of their company ("A Brief History," 2016; Vaughn, 2007)

Diversity training on sexuality, religion, ability, and ethnicity did not appear until the 1990s. Despite the decades that have passed since we implemented laws to make the workplace and society diverse and equal, many companies have issues with implementing DE&I in their culture.

According to the Runnymede Trust, there are three types of racism: individual, institutional/organisational, and systemic/structural. We must tackle each one. We can make the same distinctions for other differences.

STATISTICS

We gathered statistical data from a handful of reports. Relevant responses and conclusions are as follows and are pertinent throughout this document. In 2019, the Pew Research Center created a report: "A Changing World: Global Views on Diversity, Gender Equality, Family Life and the Importance of Religion." This report gathered statistics from around the world on questions about diversity.

69% of people believe that their country (in which they live) has become more diverse in the last two decades.

1. 68% of people believe that gender equality has improved.
2. 27% of people believe that religion holds a more important role, while 37% say it is less important and 22% believe there has been no change.
3. More people around the world are in strong favour of more gender equality, however, they are less enthusiastic about supporting overall increased diversity. This pattern was noted in many of the countries who took part.
4. Overall, 45% of people are in favour of a more diverse society compared to 23% who view diversity as a bad thing for their country.

While there has been progress in terms of DE&I in the UK, there is still much to do. Recent research by the Chartered Management Institute found male managers are blocking efforts to improve gender balance. Of the managers surveyed (1149), two-thirds believed that employing organisations could handle future challenges without gender-balanced leadership.

The Messenger and Pollard (2022) report on the NHS highlighted the fact that there are still significant problems linked to a limited approach to DE&I. "We sensed a lack of psychological safety to speak up and listen" despite progress. Minority ethnic staff (Parker, 2022) hold only sixteen percent of the FTSE (Financial Times Stock Exchange) board positions.

41% of managers (1000) surveyed by the Society of Human Resources Management (2020) reported that they were too busy to implement DE&I. They did little to act, even when there was a commitment to DE&I. Only 44% said that they had a concrete plan to address the gender imbalance.

PwC (2021) also reported similar findings in a global survey. Of those who took part, 75% stated that DE&I was a priority area, but 32% showed that there were barriers. 45% offered relevant training and 67% had affinity groups, but mainly for networking. Organisations rarely located responsibility for implementing diversity at senior levels. PwC assessed only 5% of the organisations who took part as 'having the highest level of maturity' in terms of DE&I.

DIVERSITY, EQUITY, AND INCLUSION INITIATIVES

Bersin (2020) found that organisations use traditional interventions such as diversity training, recruitment, and programmes, but that only 24% of those surveyed had diversity or inclusion goals. 40% of the companies saw the use of DE&I initiatives to mitigate possible legal repercussions for non-compliance. 25% of companies factored diversity into their leadership development and other training.

We can identify the most popular initiatives that are used as part of organisation wide programmes to enhance DE&I:

Diversity training -awareness, unconscious bias, etc.
Pro-diversity marketing material within the company, websites and in recruitment products.
Policies promoting diversity and, sometimes, positive actions.
Human resource initiatives, including targeted recruitment, e.g., first non-white senior staff member.
Diversity committees.
Employment of diversity experts as staff and managers.
Mentorship and coaching programmes.
Employee networks and employee resource groups.

These have sometimes arisen because of public pressure or a desire for social justice or recognition of the accompanying business advantage and the signals that they give internally and externally. For example, Starbucks started a one-day companywide training programme on diversity after an untoward incident involving diverse customers in one of its outlets in the US.

Research on the efficacy of these interventions points out a limited impact despite a perception that their existence makes a difference. Comprehensive and systematic reviews and meta-analyses have shown that diversity training can have a positive impact on immediate attitudes towards diversity and knowledge about other cultures, but that these decline with time. There are also mixed effects in terms of prejudice towards diverse groups. It is also possible that what respondents say about the changes they have experienced may not translate into actual behavioural adjustments. We note similar findings with implicit bias training.

Kalev et al. (2006) reviewed DE&I initiatives in the US between 1971 and 2002. They used a range of data, including federal employment records and surveys, to consider changes in managerial demographics. There were some positive shifts noted in representation at the managerial level, but training, etc. had negative effects in terms of representation. (This is one of the very few studies that used human resources data to investigate the impact of diversity initiatives.)

Diversity initiatives can also introduce a perception of fairness, which can increase a positive feeling in diverse staff but make others feel insecure. They can also lead to less support for discrimination claims brought by diverse staff and white staff may feel that it will disadvantage them if a company has a diversity programme. In the US, when there is a programme to recruit via affirmative action, sometimes employees from the overrepresented group assume incompetence in those hired and consider that is why they need extra help. (Dover et al.,2020). They suggest these factors need to be expected and dealt with when implementing diversity programmes. We have incorporated their recommendations in our suggestions below.

THE PSYCHOLOGICAL IMPACT OF DIVERSITY, EQUITY, INCLUSION AND ASSOCIATED TOXICITY

The Runnymede Trust (2022) found that 61% of the 2000 women of colour surveyed said that they had changed in terms of hair, food, what they ate and even their name to fit in. 75% of these women said that they had experienced racism at work and this, for some, led to them leaving their current posts, being blocked for promotion, etc.

Often discrimination and toxicity co-occur both in individuals and organisations, as noted by anecdotal evidence of experts who work in the UK. This can be a lethal combination for targeted staff and for the organisations, as most recently reported in the Messenger and Pollard report of leadership in the NHS. Experiencing discrimination and toxicity has a negative impact on people, including their mental health and well-being, motivation, confidence, self-doubt, ability to function and on emotions. These effects can carry on for years, especially if staff have endured silently in discriminatory and toxic work environments.

IMPLICIT BIAS

Implicit (unconscious) biases are "unconscious attitudes and stereotypes that can manifest in the workplace" (Ruhl, 2017). Employment practices are also subject to implicit bias.

Because of the plethora of information that we receive, there is a tendency to sort the world using categories. Some of these are explicit and conscious and others are not. Upbringing, family and friends, media, and the prevalent culture in which the person lives and works form and shape these biases. The League of European Research Universities (2018) described these categories as 'internalised schemas' that then influence the individual.

Implicit bias covers all areas of discrimination, from race to sexuality. The most troublesome issue with addressing implicit bias is that it is unconscious. If you're not aware that a thought or habit exists, it is difficult to address it.

DIVERSITY, EQUITY, AND INCLUSION ISSUES AND BARRIERS

"Barriers and benefits of diversity in the workplace," an article written by Western Governors University (2021), lists "problems with integration, communication issues, and resistance to change" as barriers to diversity. Not having the correct programmes in place to help with diversity training makes implementing policy very difficult, and current employees that are resistant to change can be harmful, making others feel as though they shouldn't be there or do not belong.

Renee (2019) states that "respect in the workplace, conflict among employees, alternative lifestyle acceptance, ethnic and cultural differences, gender diversity in the workplace, preventing harassment and eliminating discrimination, communication among employees, age ranges and generation gaps, disabilities and worker needs, consistency in training and practices" are the top ten diversity issues in the workplace.

Wentling (2004) selected multinational corporations in the US for a study to identify information on what assists and hinders the success of diversity initiatives. This study mentions three barriers to diversity initiatives that encompass most of the above-mentioned issues: barriers of the work environment (competing agendas, size and complexity of the corporation, and economic changes), barriers of people in corporations (people not understanding the value of diversity, people not supporting diversity, slow involvement), and barriers of diversity initiatives (hard to evaluate, difficult to show a return on investment, organizational policies interfering with diversity initiatives).

Companies may become overenthusiastic about their own success, feeling as though they have succeeded just because they have done something "first." However, those who are the first- such as "the first woman to become a director"- must contend with much stereotyping and other problems. Firsts in diversity are often alone and can be on the receiving end of aggression, expected to perform above expectations in a harsh environment and must ignore hostility and harmful comments (Nordell, 2021). A single initiative rarely indicates successful inclusion across an organisation.

FACILITATING AND INCORPORATING DIVERSITY, EQUITY, AND INCLUSION.

This section is based on the above discussion and incorporates identified key factors to ensure success in implementation. We include recommendations for intervention. Again, these are based on research or seminal guidance.

An intentional understanding of diversity issues

To address these, we must first acknowledge that they exist, that the system set in place was not made to be inclusive, and therefore it fails people from diverse backgrounds. Badenoch (2022) lists three necessary steps:

1. Acknowledging failings where they have occurred.
2. Improving actions, behaviours and systems that led to the loss of trust.
3. Honesty and transparency in communication from government, its delivery agencies and from other stakeholders including business, the media and civil society".

It is important to listen to input from your team. However, people have a desire to avoid conflict and may not speak up. To address this issue, you can incorporate silent voting or anonymous brainstorming, which are "two ways to consider all ideas and to prevent mediocre ideas from taking the spotlight" (McKinsey & Company, n.d.). Giving everyone a chance to speak their mind, even if it is in private, can help to identify and solve previously unnoticed problems.

It is crucial to be inclusive and adopt an intersectional approach. So that all employees feel included regardless of difference. This must be clear at all levels of the organisation, from work practices to operations, policy, and strategy.

Education

Looking back to "Author Talks: Forge your power," Purushothaman talks about how her novel, "The First, the Few, the Only: How Women of Color Can Redefine Power in Corporate America" describes what it is like to be a woman of colour while also answering questions about diversity (McKinsey & Company, 2022). She points out we do not design many things, like planes, with women or mothers in mind. Anecdotal evidence suggests that women given positions of power aren't happy or haven't received what leadership promised. Partly because, much like planes, they did not design the corporate world with women of colour in mind. It is important that companies work just as hard to keep women and women of colour as they do men.

This is where education comes in. Just as people read works by others who think differently than them to open another lane of thinking, so they should read things from the point of view of a minority to understand the struggles and thoughts of that minority and educate themselves on the historical issues surrounding diversity to further learn how they can change their behaviour or area to be more inclusive.

Learning about and reducing unconscious bias

We have mentioned that one of the primary issues in addressing implicit bias is that it is unconscious. To address unconscious bias, we must take active steps- through adjusting our perspective via training and education (Ruhl, 2020). When we adjust our perspective, we allow ourselves to see and consider how others may feel about a situation.

In and out of the workplace, training and educating ourselves about our biases are the most active steps we can take. Though changing our perspective can help open our eyes to discrimination, incorporating bias training into our programme or life, and educating others integrates change into our routine. In fact, "Education is crucial. Understanding what implicit biases are, how they can arise, and how to recognize them in ourselves and others are all incredibly important in working towards overcoming such biases."

Once we learn about implicit bias and take the steps to remove it from our habits, we should then convey the risks of it to others and help them develop habits like the ones we have implemented into our routine and thought process to facilitate changes in others' unconscious bias habits (Tslpursky, 2020).

The importance of workplace culture

In the "Global Culture Survey 2021: The link between culture and competitive advantage" report written by the Katzenback Center; companies that amplify their cultural traits could be a source of competitive advantage. We define culture as "the self-sustaining pattern of behaviours that determine how things are done" (PwC, n.d.). They compiled the results of several surveys in their report of international responses comprising the UK, the USA, the Netherlands, Switzerland, South Africa, Singapore, Russia, Malaysia, Japan, Australia, and more. They found that

67% of respondents agreed with the statement that "our organization's culture is an important topic on the agenda of our company's senior leadership". 81% see their work culture as a source of competitive advantage.

"Purposeful management of culture" with consistency is important. Employees need to know what to expect from their organization, such as making sure that the company culture embodies DE&I. The culture must also promote and enable psychological safety.

Evidence shows that diverse teams outperform less diverse teams. However, often diverse teams underperform because of challenges, e.g. poor communication with them. To address this, work environments must contain a large degree of psychological safety: "a shared belief that team members will not be rejected or embarrassed for speaking up with their ideas, questions, or concerns" (Bresman & Edmondson, 2022). A study showed that teams that rated high in psychological safety had a positive association between performance and diversity. We can facilitate psychologically safe environments through framing, inquiry, and bridging boundaries.

Framing helps members of a team "reach a common understanding of the work and the context." For example, rather than having team meetings that only update attendees, sharing ideas and information should be a goal rather than a passive expectation. We should invite people to join the conversation and make room for raising questions and offering new ideas.

We should frame difference as a source of value when diverse people speak. Alternative perspectives allow for a greater overall understanding of the problem or issues at hand.

Inquiry is encouraging people to contribute their ideas. When working in a diverse team, there are a greater number of perspectives, so inquiry can lead others to come up with, or articulate, their own ideas. To encourage this, leadership should use "open questions" and "questions that build shared ownership and causality" in team meetings. These should have no predetermined answer and "reflect the complexity of integrating diverse views" rather than those that lead to blame for the person's contribution to the challenge or issue.

We can accomplish bridging boundaries by asking task-relevant questions such as "what do you want to accomplish?" and "What are you up against?" This can help team members understand one another's objectives and expertise and then work together more effectively.

Ikiler spoke on a panel discussing gender in business and human rights and explained that diversity and inclusion need to be made a part of the company's culture rather than being adopted through a "tick-box approach" ("Organizations Need," 2021). Nor should there be a "one size fits all" approach. Different areas should define their own initiatives for diversity and inclusion based on locality and cultural differences.

Integrating a workforce and giving equal space requires educating staff about why diversity, equity and inclusion is important and what a company stands to gain not just financially but also in work culture. Everyone brings something different to the table because of differences in life experience, priorities, and educational journeys.

Interrupting bias

"How the Best Bosses Interrupt Bias on Their Teams" (2019), explains how a leader can avoid the mistakes that lead to ineffective bias-prevention programmes. We note that in everyday work interactions, there are four ways bias can have an impact:

1. Some groups must prove themselves more than others.
2. A narrower range of behaviours is allowed and expected from some groups than others.
3. The commitment and competence of women with children is questioned more often, and people can look down on them for being too focused on their careers.
4. Disadvantaged groups can find themselves at odds with each other because of a refusal to assimilate or different methods of assimilation.

We must understand first how biases function in the workplace and then recognize when and where they arise. True diversity must be the goal when hiring, more than simply increasing numbers of certain diverse groups. Implicit bias can lead to harsher or unequal judgement of out-groups. When hiring, the criteria list for eligibility for the position should be set and not altered. Limit referral hiring, as this can lead to the perpetual continuation of homogeneity within an organization. Interview based on agreed competencies, and every person interviewed should be asked the same list of questions or be given an equally difficult level of problem to solve.

Hiring should be active and reach out to, or partner with, women and minority groups. To recruit from them can lead an organization away from a monotonic past. Major companies such as Google have implemented this, partnering with historically black colleges (HBCUs) and Hispanic-serving institutions.

Another issue is "office housework." With administrative tasks and cleaning, women are more likely to be expected to handle these, with women of colour more supposed to complete this work than white women. With this come several biases, manifestations, and workplace issues, including the frequent interruption of women in meetings by men, that a man with an equal level of expertise to his female counterparts is likely to be seen as more influential.

To address the housework issue: don't leave administrative tasks to volunteers. We should create a fair rotation system to keep women and people of colour from feeling pressured into those positions.

We also give some groups more menial responsibilities while tasking just as-experienced co-workers' with high-value projects. We should fairly allocate high value project tasks using logic and reason. Favouritism and nepotism should not be permitted. If we see someone behave with bias, then steps should be taken to help them realise this and then address it.

We can also address bias in work practices. Meetings should occur at convenient times and places. They ought to be facilitated so that all who are present feel they can speak and contribute.

There ought to be fair and equal access to senior personnel without bias or conditions. Similarly, performance appraisal systems need to be operationalised so that all are clear on goals and expectations and there is trust in how managers use them to help staff grow and develop rather than as a threat or punishment.

Action plans that start from the top and trickle-down

Wentling (2004) identified factors that assist the success of diversity initiatives, "top management support, endorsement, and commitment" and "recognizing that diversity is more than just an HR issue" are two of the three most frequently mentioned factors cited by study participants. One study said, "Our diversity initiatives have been successful because we have a culture that supports diversity. Diversity is part of the culture from the highest to the very bottom levels. The value of diversity is something that is communicated throughout the entire organisation, just as with any other business strategy, such as quality management. Senior management supported from the beginning their initiatives. Diversity must start from the top and be recognized as imperative to a business."

Sancier-Sultan & Zavjalov (2022) recommend a strategically implemented plan to incorporate diversity and inclusion. The steps are:

1. *"Treat sociocultural diversity as a strategic goal for top management."* It cannot only be DE&I departments that care about diversity, it must come from the top and not just be an idea or a belief, but an actual programme. "Changes to promote socio-cultural diversity should be rolled out at every level of the corporate hierarchy." There must be corporate-diversity indicators, an evolution of HR management process, and support from leadership.

2. *"Introducing clear indicators."* We must focus on efforts. To increase diversity, there must be clear quantitative monitors to measure it, such as the proportion of diversity in new hires, management, and each level of business.

3. *"An action plan."* The plan must be a thorough roadmap, not just policy.

4. *"Develop an inclusive work culture."* The diversity plan needs to be embedded in the company and encouraged rather than just approved.

When implementing diversity in an institution or organization, there must be measurable results. Results need to be assessable to know if the initiative is helpful or not. (Petersen, 2021).

Different people with different backgrounds have varying preferences. Preferences and boundaries are especially noticeable when considering generation gaps in the workplace. "For the first time in modern history, there are five generations in the workplace. We each exhibit "unique personality traits and values" (Waldman, 2021). However, a lack of knowledge about preferences and boundaries can cause conflict or a lack of communication due to discomfort. It is important that we bridge the gap between generations, especially since there are several benefits to multi-generational work because of different values and traits. To allow for equal opportunity in generational disparities, we must:

1. "Challenge harmful stereotypes"
2. "Openly communicate preferences": Whether one prefers to communicate through emailing, texting, or calling, or if someone has a work style to which they adhere.
3. "Respect boundaries": There is more open space to talk about diversity, mental illness, and gender roles. Younger generations are said to be more comfortable talking about previously taboo topics, so it is important to respect who is comfortable with which topic.
4. "No favouritism." Make sure that, though you may like a particular person or employee, you are not favouring them over others. Be aware of affinity bias.

In implementing diversity, several sources have stated that taking steps with intention is an important stride toward the success of the initiative. When looking into implementing DE&I into a business, learning about the plans other businesses have made and how successful they are is important to determine the steps to take and mistakes to avoid.

The International Standard (ISO) for Diversity, Equity, and Inclusion is a guidance document and actionable guide for organizations ("Human Resource Management", 2021).To implement DE&I, we note there are important prerequisites in this guide: recognizing diversity, governing effectively, acting accountably (actions should be ethically and socially responsible), working inclusively, communicating inclusively (understanding that people have different communication needs and acting in a manner that works with these needs), and advocating and championing for diversity and inclusion. Take these active steps early in implementing DE&I, however, if we omit them, it is never too late to use them.

SUMMARY AND RECOMMENDATIONS

It is laudable that there has been progress in incorporating diversity, equity, inclusion into the fabric of organisations and business. We need much more to be truly inclusive of all, regardless of difference.

Here are some suggestions, based on our analysis of the research and the guidance we considered.

We require a wide and inclusive definition of diversity, equity, and inclusion and suggestions on how to operationalise it. We need an increased awareness and recognition of the need for DE&I in attitudes. Associated changes in behaviours that mirror the aspirations and vision of diversity should accompany this.

Communication to employees should be respectful of the varying diverse needs and preferences for interaction.

Organisational culture should facilitate the above and encourage psychological safety for all concerned.

Identify and address toxic behaviours and cultures. Similarly, barriers to diversity within an organisation need to be identified, as well as the recognition that there will be variations in how inclusive and welcoming personnel are. Some will be positive, others reluctant, and a few could be obstructive.

Governance and leadership should incorporate and advocate for DE&I. They should be prepared to take the risks and embed DE&I in all aspects of the organisation. All efforts need to be clarified by measurable goals and outcomes.

An inclusive approach to learning and development is required. This should incorporate awareness training, and plans, post training should support this, to assist behavioural change.

Internal justice systems (reporting of untoward behaviour, investigation, mediation, etc.) need to be supported, bearing in mind the need for confidentiality. Both employees and leadership should trust them.

All aspects of the human resource management life cycle must include DE&I principles throughout: workforce planning, remuneration, recruitment, onboarding, learning and development, performance management, succession planning, workforce mobility and cessation of employment.

All operational policies and strategies need to provide an arena for the facilitation and operationalisation of DE&I. DE&I also needs to be factored into products and services offered, development and design, procurement, and supply chains, as well as external stakeholder relationships.

This is a massive but necessary agenda. It is vital to work towards this if we are really to progress DE&I in business. Diverse staff have waited long enough.

REFERENCES

Badenoch, K. (2022, March 17). *Inclusive Britain: Government response to the commission on race and ethnic disparities.* GOV. UK. Retrieved June 27, 2022, from https://www.gov.uk/government/publications/inclusive-britain-action-plan-government-response-to-the-commission-on-race-and-ethnic-disparities/inclusive-britain-government-response-to-the-commission-on-race-and-ethnic-disparities

Bersin, J. (2020) *Elevating equity: the real story of diversity and equity.* www.joshbersin.com

Brazen. (2016, February 17). *A brief history of diversity in the workplace [infographic].* Retrieved June 27, 2022, from https://www.brazen.com/resources/a-brief-history-of-diversity-in-the-workplace-infographic

Bresman, H., & Edmondson, A. C. (2022, March 17). *Research: To Excel, Diverse Teams Need Psychological Safety.* hbr. org. Retrieved June 27, 2022, from https://hbr.org/2022/03/research-to-excel-diverse-teams-need-psychological-safety

Chartered Management Institute (2022) *Gender Balance.* https://www.managers.org.uk/about-cmi/media-centre/press-office/press-releases/cmi-research-reveals-chasm-between-male-and-female-managers-views-on-need-for-more-gender-balanced-leadership-and-opportunities%ef%bf%bc/

Crenshaw, K. (1989) *Demarginalizing the Intersection of Race and Sex: A Black Feminist Critique of Antidiscrimination Doctrine, Feminist Theory and Antiracist Politics.* University of Chicago Legal Forum. Volume 1989. Issue 1, pp. 139-167

Dong, S. (2021, June 2). *The history and growth of the diversity, equity, and Inclusion Profession.* Global Research and Consulting Group Insights. Retrieved June 27, 2022, from https://insights.grcglobalgroup.com/the-history-and-growth-of-the-diversity-equity-and-inclusion-profession/#:~:text=Workplace%20diversity%20training%20first%20emerged,known%20histories%20of%20racial%20discrimination

Dover, T.L, Kaiser, C.R. and Major, B (2020). *Mixed Signals: The Unintended effects of diversity initiatives.* Social Issues and Policy Review, Vol. 14, No. 1, 2020, pp. 152--181 DOI: 10.1111/sipr.12059

Erickson, W. A., von Schrader, S., Bruyère, S. M., & VanLooy, S. A. (2014). *The employment environment: Employer perspectives, policies, and practices regarding the employment of persons with disabilities.* Rehabilitation Counseling Bulletin, 57(4), 195-208.

Global Diversity Practice (2019) *What is Diversity & Inclusion?* (2019, October 25). Retrieved June 27, 2022, from https://global-diversitypractice.com/what-is-diversity-inclusion/

Grindstaff, L. (2022). *Barriers to Inclusion: Social Roots and Current Concerns*. In: Bisson, L.F., Grindstaff, L., Brazil-Cruz, L., Barbu, S.J. (eds) Uprooting Bias in the Academy. Springer, Cham. https://doi.org/10.1007/978-3-030-85668-7_2

Gyimah, M., Azad, Z., Begum, S. Kapoor, A, Ville, L. Henderson, A., Dey, M. (2022). *The Myth of Meritocracy for Women of Colour in the Workplace*. Runnymede Trust.

Harvard Business Review Analytic Services (2021) *Creating a Culture of Diversity, Equity, and Inclusion: Real Progress Requires Sustained Commitment*. Harvard Business Review Analytic Services.

ISO. International Standard Issue 30415. *Human Resource Management- Diversity and Inclusion,* no.1. (May 2021).

League of European Research Universities (2018). *Implicit bias in academia: a challenge to the meritocratic principle and to women's careers-and what to do about it.* Advice Paper No 23. January 2018

McKinsey & Company. (2022, March 3). *Author talks: Forge Your Power*. McKinsey & Company. Retrieved June 27, 2022, from https://www.mckinsey.com/featured-insights/mckinsey-on-books/author-talks-forge-your-power

McKinsey & Company. (n.d.). *Leading off: Tackling Complex Problems: A Leader's Guide*. Global management consulting. Retrieved June 27, 2022, from https://www.mckinsey.com/~/media/mckinsey/email/leadingoff/2022/04/04/2022-04-04b.html

General Sir Messenger, G. and Dame Pollard, L. (2022). *Health and social care review: leadership for a collaborative and inclusive future. Independent Report*. www.gov.uk

GroupM (2021*). Organizations Need to Make Diversity and Inclusion a Fundamental Part of Their Culture*. GroupM. (2021, December 1). Retrieved June 27, 2022, from https://www.groupm.com/newsroom/organizations-need-to-make-diversity-and-inclusion-a-fundamental-part-of-their-culture/

Nordell, J. (2021, November 1). *The end of bias: A beginning: The Science and practice of overcoming unconscious bias*. Next Big Idea Club. Retrieved June 27, 2022, from https://nextbigideaclub.com/magazine/end-bias-beginning-science-practice-overcoming-unconscious-bias-bookbite/30352/

OpenLearn. (n.d.). *Working in Diverse Teams*. Retrieved June 27, 2022, from https://www.open.edu/openlearn/money-business/working-diverse-teams/content-section-overview?active-tab=content-tab

Parker, Sir J. (2022) *Improving the Ethnic Diversity of UK Boards. An Update Report from the Parker Review*. UK Department for Business, Energy, and Industrial Strategy

Petersen, K. (2021, June 14). *4 Factors to Consider When Promoting Diversity in the Workplace*. Rasmussen University. Retrieved June 27, 2022, from https://www.rasmussen.edu/degrees/business/blog/diversity-in-the-workplace/

Pew Research Center. (2014, August 27). *Global Religious Diversity*. Pew Research Center's Religion & Public Life Project. Retrieved June 27, 2022, from https://www.pewresearch.org/religion/2014/04/04/global-religious-diversity/

Poushter, J., Fetterrolf, J and Tamir, C. (2019) *A Changing World: Global Views on Diversity, Gender Equality, Family Life and the Importance of Religion People see more diversity and gender equality happening but say family ties have weakened.* Pew Research Centre

PricewaterhouseCoopers. (2017). *Global Diversity and Inclusion Survey*. PwC. Retrieved June 27, 2022, from https://www.pwc.com/gx/en/services/people-organisation/global-diversity-and-in-clusion-survey.html

PwC. (n.d.). *Global Culture Survey 2021 Report*. PwC. Retrieved June 27, 2022, from https://www.pwc.com/gx/en/issues/upskill-ing/global-culture-survey-2021/global-culture-survey-2021-re-port.html

Renee, M. (2019, March 6). *Top 10 diversity issues at work*. Small Business - Chron.com. Retrieved June 28, 2022, from https://smallbusiness.chron.com/top-10-diversity-issues-work-24939.html

Rosencrance, L. (2022) *Diversity, equity, and inclusion*. https://www.techtarget.com/searchhrsoftware/definition/diversity-equity-and-inclusion-DEI

Roos, E. (2022*). Understanding privilege.* In Healthy Leadership and Organisations: Beyond the shadow side. Eliatamby, A. (Editor)

Ruhl, C. (2020, July 1). *Implicit or Unconscious Bias.* Simply Psychology. Retrieved June 27, 2022, from https://www.simply-psychology.org/implicit-bias.html

Sancier-Sultan, S., & Zavjalov, S. (2022, April 15). *Beyond Gender: Promoting Diversity in French Companies.* McKinsey & Company. Retrieved June 27, 2022, from https://www.mckinsey.com/featured-insights/diversity-and-inclusion/beyond-gender-promoting-diversity-in-french-companies.

Schein, Edgar H.; Bennis, Warren G. (1965) *Personal and organizational change through group methods: the laboratory approach. New York: Wiley.*

Society of Human Resource Managers with Harvard Business Review Analytical Services. (2021). *Creating a culture of diversity, equity, and inclusion. Real progress requires sustained commitment.* SHRM with HBR.

Tslpursky, G. (2020, July 13). *What is unconscious bias (and how you can defeat it).* Psychology Today. Retrieved June 27, 2022, from https://www.psychologytoday.com/us/blog/intentional-insights/202007/what-is-unconscious-bias-and-how-you-can-defeat-it

Vaughn, B. E. (2007). *The History of Diversity Training & Its Pioneers.* Strategic Diversity & Inclusion Management Magazine, pp. 11 – 16, Vol.1, Issue 1, Spring 2007. DTUI.com Publications Division

Vornholt, K., Uitdewilligen, S., & Nijhuis, F. J. (2013). *Factors Affecting the Acceptance of People with Disabilities at Work: A Literature Review.* Journal of occupational rehabilitation, 23(4), 463-475.Waldman, E. (2021, August 21). How to Manage a Multi-Generational Team. Harvard Business Review. Retrieved June 27, 2022, from https://hbr.org/2021/08/how-to-manage-a-multi-generational-team

Wentling, R. M. (2004). *Factors That Assist and Barriers That Hinder the Success of Diversity Initiatives in Multinational Corporations.* Human Resource Development International, 7(2), 165-180.

Western Governors University. (2021, September 23). *Barriers and benefits of diversity in the workplace.* Western Governors University. Retrieved June 27, 2022, from https://www.wgu.edu/blog/barriers-benefits-diversity-workplace1906.html#close

Williams, J. C., & Mihaylo, S. (2022, February 11). *How the Best Bosses Interrupt Bias on Their Teams.* Harvard Business Review. Retrieved June 28, 2022, from https://hbr.org/2019/11/how-the-best-bosses-interrupt-bias-on-their-teams

Printed in Great Britain
by Amazon

17909676R00040